Published by:
Ulysses Press
P.O. Box 3440
Berkeley, CA 94703
www.ulyssespress.com

ISBN: 978-1-61243-763-7
Library of Congress Control Number: 2017959022

Printed in the United States
10 12 14 16 18 10 20 19 17 15 13 11

Acquisitions editor: Casie Vogel
Proofreader: Shayna Keyles
Cover design: Sarah Lee
Interior design and layout: what!design @ whatweb.com
Illustrations: Liz Emirzian on pages 5, 6, 9, 11, 16, 28, 34, 36, 39, 52, 61, 65, 69, 72, 75, 77, 96, 106, 107; heart page 3 © inspiron 1525/shutterstock.com

2Fish

(a poetry book)

Jhené Aiko Efuru Chilombo

to you, from me... with love ♡ —Jhené

1Fish

in the past
she was angry
in the future
she was scared
but alive in the moment
is where
she's aware

2Fish

i loved you
then the wind blew
it is simple
these are changes
we are meant for
they're essential

ike a child in the womb
ith no room to grow
n the wild in the nude
I'm confused and cold
hen you show me all the
hings I could NEVER SEE
It's a DOOMED REALITY
~~THAT~~ I can not beLIEVE

WHAT YOU'VE DONE TO ME

I'm not having a good time
YOU WERE SPOSE to get me high
But you took me out my
                    mind
WAY DOWN TO THE OTHER
                    SIDE

BAD TRIP

Becoming my friend
coming to an end
it's not the
worse thing tha
can happen

Imagine
Being trapped in
a nightmare, waking up in
~~a day dream, the so~~
~~scared to be trapped a~~
~~stranger~~ thing
~~freedom~~ WHEN
AWAKE AND AR
AWAITING
FOR THE DAY
DREAM

3Fish

it was never love
it was not even close

it was closest
to hopeless

it was hell
at the most

it was mouths wide open
and minds that were closed

it was dead
it was over

chopped liver

burnt toast

4Fish

do you know what really sucks?

when you swallow a pill

and that pill gets stuck

and you wait for the feels

but the feels won't come

cuz the pain
of the pill
in your throat

makes it numb

focused on the pain
you miss the whole high

you forget the whole feeling
of wanting to die

cuz now you're like
"please, pill! please pass by!"

and you sob and you cry

then it all gets worse...

now you're high
and you're crying
and your throat really hurts

On the pursuit of perfection

her

She waved goodbye to the m~~ir~~

to her face as she knew ~~i~~

And woke up with a pain in

her side

With a tube running through

with a drain for the fluid

AND ~~WITH~~ the same ~~BROUGHT~~ BLIND PR~~IDE~~

That made her do it.

~~THE SAME~~ *WAS THE* BLIND PRIDE THAT

WOULD HELP HER GET THROUGH

~~ABCDEFGHIJK~~ The minisule alteration

WOULD soon be revealed ~~...~~

AND NOW ~~...~~ FALSE HOP~~E~~

TOLD HER SHE WOULD BE

HEALED

ON THE INSIDE, FROM THE

~~INSIDE~~

T FROM THE OUTSIDE, Looking

~~BACK~~ IT WAS OBVIOUS THE PAIN
WOULD WORSEN
AS THE REALITY SET IN.

WHEN THE MONTHS TURNED TO
YEARS
AND ~~HER THE~~ REFLECTION ONLY REFLECTED
HER ~~FEARS~~
THEN THE WORRY, AND THE SHAME
WOULD SHOW UP ON HER FACE

ON
~~AT~~ THE PURSUIT OF perfection
one could say,

THERE IS no such thing
you will lose your way

Say Hello to your SELF
and you're welcome
to your TRUE

ENDLESS
RIDICULOUS
PURSUIT OF PERFECTION.

5Fish

the wave was afraid
for a moment there

when the momentum
forced her in the air

she was scared

fearing that this
may just be the end

but then
the wind,
(a friend)

showed her the way

told her she'd carry her
through night 'til the day

through beautiful canyons...
past forests and streets

past mountains
and canyons
and valleys
and peaks

as they passed the cove
and rose to new heights
the wave could then see

(and much to her delight)

she need not worry
of returning to sea

cause life was everlasting

and she
was free

6Fish

i was
a sunken ship

a drunken sip
of something thick...

and then i took a trip

there was no captain
but you were my anchor

there were poisons and demons
and rhymes with no reasons

and strangers

but there was no danger

Grampy called me "Penny"
but you taught me i was plenty

and you taught me that to be complete
that you have to be empty

and free from all the miseries
and energies that hinder me

you brought me to my inner peace
you taught me it was meant for me

until we meet again
my friend

it ends how it begins

3:16 (in the car)

27

10

$2 + 7 = 9$

If not you
than someones
like you

9 is completion

DEATH OF SELF

REST OF SELF

Rest assure

In over my head

Envy ~~crossed out~~

the DEAD

Multiples   Multiples
Multiples   Multiples
Multiples   Multiples   Multiples
Multiples   Multiples   Multiples

You have everything you need
to do anything you want.
And what do you do?
Nothing.

7Fish

it was written in the stars

it was written in the scars
on her arm

in her palms
where she wept

in her bed
where she slept

or

hardly slept at all

what a doll

with her skin made
of plastic
and tears made
of acid

she could not hide the
tragic
damage
of sadness

that burned through her pores
and straight to her core

where she learned to keep quiet
and not cry anymore

8Fish

no wonder

the mind begins to wander...

time is running over
as i am going under...

i am getting older

(but cooler)

can you please share my stories
when i'm gone?

Close minds don't get fed
JUDGED BY EYES
↓ ↓↓

JUDGING OTHERS, JUDGING OTHERS
STUDY OTHERS, STUDY OTHERS
STEADY
DEAD MEAT

YOU ARE WHAT YOU EAT!
DEAD MEET!
YOU GROW WHAT YOU FEED
DON'T FEED THE FEARS?
NO, FEED THEM
THEN FREE THEM,
BECOME THEM
BE THEM
SEE THEM AS FRIENDS
AND THEN SEND THEM ON
THEIR WAY

9Fish

crazy how
i can stare

into empty space

and see his smile...
i see his face...

crystal clear as day

i close my eyes
and hear his voice

i hear him say my name

and we start to talk
and I have to ask
"been wondering
how do you feel?"

i say, "I'm afraid that i will forget you"

and he says,

"I'm afraid you never will"

10Fish

who ever said
"fools rush in"
was wrong

the dumb thing to do
is to wait
too long

because laters
and eventually's
aren't promised
to come

all we ever really have

is this moment

just one

and moment
to moment
it's new
and it's young

and waiting is death
to what could have begun

"When you get it
RIGHT,"
YOU DIE,
HE said
envying the DEAD.

11Fish

fill the void w/
filled prescriptions

want to end it all

what has led to
this decision?

i am trippin balls

12Fish

so, you think I'm pretty...
you think i'm too skinny

but

who asked you?
for your fucking opinion?

13Fish

new highs
followed by
new lows

all for the balance

I suppose

14Fish

it was
so real
i was physically shaking
the vibrations were waking
like waves when they're breaking
i embodied the shore
i embody, the sure
i was body, the pure
i am body, but more ·

i am body
no more

i am all

i was
small
but my energy
was TALL
too bright to call
or name it a thing
too expansive
too massive
a mass never seen

so i cut my self open
as ego bled out
as eagles stretched wings
and the heavens sing loud

with the earth ripping open
i was shot through its womb
pass my past
pass my future
pass demons
and gloom

pass the fire
they teach us
pass the devil
himself
i shot right past Satan
speeding bullet to hell ·

but the speed was so brilliant
i did not stop just there
i went way down to realms
that no one NEW was there

it was carefully guarded
by the darkest of skies
by a darkness so pretty
and a silence so nice

heard my Grampy call "Penny"
and my brother laugh twice
but i couldn't see any
there were no i's to cry

knew i must have been home
there was no sense of self
and the air was so calm
there were no thoughts to dwell

and my senses so strong
with no judge to condemn me

annihilation of self
i was gone
i was empty

i was free
i was all
there was no cause for pity

and my eyes were his eyes, and her eyes...so many...

and to put it simply

i found heaven within thee...
depths of the death
of the myth
that i am "me"

"Good Things
Should be
Shared."

~~ARE~~

Remember when we
slept together, but DIDN'T
"SLEEP together"?
Your HEAD was touching mine
Like our minds WERE ~~&~~ intertwined
And I DREAMED OF YOU
~~OOOOOOOOOO~~
~~TODAY ALRIGHT~~ THAT NIGHT...
WHAT A DREAM COME TRUE
TO WAKE UP AND SEE
YOU STILL ....
TO SEE YOU THERE,
THEN SEE YOU HERE...
~~OOOOOOOOOOOO~~
~~OOOOO~~ ~~OOOO~~ SO REAL & ~~COMPLETE~~

15Fish

Ark To Agartha - THE PLAY

BRIGHT ROOM, BLINDING LIGHTS

The girl is alone w/ EGO behind her

EGO: you are not enough

(The girl believes it, begins to feel... takes a pill to relieve it)

EGO: you are at fault

(The dosage increases)

EGO: here's what you've done

ABRUBT DARKNESS

(we see it)

(there are only dark figures, like shadows of the past
reenacting past actions... the girl cant get passed)

(near over dose, wakes up to war outside)

Boy 1: we're the only lovers left alive!

16Fish

i shouted to the stars
but there were no answers
i called out to God

you were there

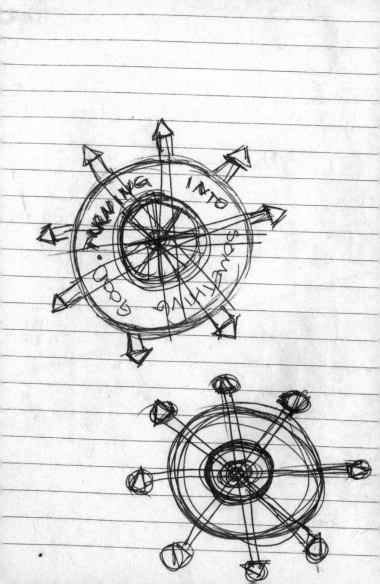

17Fish

if u say it's love
but do not feel free
it can't be the thing
you claim it to be

18Fish

i'm sorry I'm not what you're use to
i can't hide my flaws

i don't choose to

i am not in your box
of what's in
or what's hot

does me being me
confuse you?

i am sorry you don't think I'm beautiful

i'm sorry your mom did not hug you
and your dad did not teach you to love you

but there are reasons and ways
to overcome hate

and the first step would be
to choose to

BUBBLES

Rings?
What do RINGS REALLY MEAN?
Just
I keep changing my mind
Just
I keep changing my kind
I must be playing

WHEN SOMETHING IS
BROKEN.
YOU DONT THROW IT AWA
HAVE TO FIND
7-19-15

A WAY

19Fish

hot shower
for an hour

i surrender all my power

i will cower
in the corner
(on the floor)

i will drown my inner coward
and the demons i've encountered
lying down between the tile
and the door

20Fish

i was born knowing
exactly where i'm going
in the city of
lost angels

where people travel
to settle down into
their fantasy webs
that are tangled

i am from a land
where everyone comes
to pretend to be
something they dreamed up

while me and my fellow
homeschooled kids
pray to the stars to be beamed up

~~2~~ 2 Fish ~~~~

~~the path of the creatures~~

with one foot in ~~the~~ water
and one foot on the land
She followed her path
on the shore
As planned

2 FISH

greater than no one <
lesser than no one > 0

21Fish

afraid to say
"i'd like it very much if you'd stay and lose sleep with me tonight"
not my misery needing company
it is just me
i might
not feel lonely on most days
but tonight reminds me of Summer
reminds me that i have and am not a kid now
and that i am missing a brother
go to call a sister
his name is right with hers
i haven't deleted his number
i don't want to say all he meant to me
and have you say how you wish you'd met him
i don't want to cry and confess
how i feel as time passes by
i'll forget him
and you look at me like
"I wish I could help"
but your father was there
and you've always had help
and your brother's still calling
and you've always been dealt
with aces and high hands and silver fucking platters
the audacity
the nerve
to ask me "whats the matter?"
and if i were really in the mood to discuss
i would tell you how i
never felt like enough
how i was the ugly one
hated the mirror
and took lots of pills that one night trying to kill her
if i had the energy
i'd tell you the truth
that i haven't been happy since I was in school
like elementary
even then
shit was crazy
the youngest

but toughest
i was never the baby
so i don't want your pity
or your words
or advice
i'd just like it very much if
you lost sleep with me tonight

Hello Ego
(freestyle)   May 17, 2015

I should stop drinkin

I should stop smokin

I need to focus   I am
~~I have been~~ chosen
~~Heaven~~
They say I'm the Pope
That's why

I am the   lotus flowing
lotus   bogus

I am floatin boasting
I am growin, Despite

I should let go of
all these notions

But I got ~~these~~ them vicodin
verses
For all these bitches you
~~hurt~~ when
you tell em you fuckin
w/ me

22Fish

two word prayer:
thank you

23Fish

July 19, 2012

last Summer,
we were dying together
why did I stay?
why did you go?

my big brother,
has it really been that long?
since we shared our ideas,
and sang our favorite songs?

how do you feel now?
where did you go?

was it really necessary that i lose you
in order to grow?

well, what about our plans?
and who's gonna make me laugh?
i wasted so many days looking for what i already had

now i'm searching for a brother's love
in every single man

i didn't want to leave you
rather it be me than you
in that bed
tube in head
staring at the corner of the room

the same room we grew up in
playing mortal combat
or street fighter
i always got the two confused

you would let me play, and claim i was winning...
but the controller wouldn't be connected
i figured it out one day

there use to be two doors in that room
one led to the front of the house
the other to the kitchen

our younger cousins will never know about that second door

we always said that Grandma Essie's house was a special place
and you got to spend your last days there
you are the lucky one

i always left you alone
we should have been together more often when it was just the two of us
downstairs
but we had our own friends
and I was always with my boyfriend
but you were always my best friend

i just thought we'd have more time
I thought that it would turn around

i miss you most days
some days I feel more close to you than ever
but
the summer isn't the summer without my brother
we should be at Venice beach
or the observatory
walking to Puerto Nuevo for nachos
or 7/11 for slurpees
bonfires,
scary movies
there's a swimming pool where i stay now
i wish i could invite you over
are you everywhere now?
or no where?
if you send for me,
i will go there.
i'm alone here
can you feel my kisses on your picture?

i can see you still
running up the hill with your afro and basketball
somehow you always missed the bus and i made it
i always told the driver to wait for you
but most times he didn't

do you hear these thoughts?
where are you?
I left my joy and any sense of hope in San Francisco
a year ago today
when they called us and told us that you had went your way
you waited for us to leave
so that we wouldn't be there to see
screaming, crying

pulling over on the side of the freeway
i could of ran in that traffic right then and there.
but i froze
we should have never left you
to come here
to the place your favorite football team plays
to the place where our uncle was dying of the same disease

they put your ear to the phone and our big sister told you we were coming
home

did you hear her?
we couldn't catch a flight
so we drove

the longest drive of our lives
i could not close my eyes
until i saw you
until i saw that it was true

early morning we arrived
through the side gate
to the back door
through the kitchen we used to make special coffee drinks before
there was a a such thing as Starbucks

through the living room where we use to build tents out of blankets
and couches

where we watched Dave Chapelle's first stand up special together and
declared him our favorite

to the front room
where you were
so handsome
so peaceful

i held my breath waiting to see you take another
but you did not

where did you go?
do i really have to grow up without you?
am I really alive without you?

are you in the stars?
is there a God?
do you walk with him?

is he a she?
is she in me?
will we ever talk again?

is it strange that I cant wait to meet my fate,
just to see your face
again?

Miyagi Ayo Hasani Chilombo.
i love you to infinity.
- your baby sister
7/19/13

Oh boy, Imma have to call
them boys on ya
Auw damn, I'mma have to call
Somethin must be really wrong
w/ you ...
Why can't you just tell the trut
now ...
Yes ya mama did she raised
fool, wow!
WTF did you learn in that sch
house?
To chase them thrills, chasin th
taking pills, in the hills, SLAUSON
Overhills, might get you killed ..
Not welcome round them parts
Do not run your mouth no more
I can't protect you no more
It's out of my hands for su
You should of called me
Why you never call me?

24Fish

i am the eye of the storm

i am calm when the earth quakes beneath me

standing my ground
with my roots
gripping deeply

telling the truth
when need be

but never too loud
i don't have to shout

honest and modest
and proud

25Fish

"not the kind of pretty she thought she'd grow to be" excerpt from
"the girl who wanted plastic surgery" (by me)

TRIPS

Pill trip ~~write~~
Guilt trip
BAD TRIP
EGO TRIP
Relation Ship
Ark to AGARTHA

Acid Trip?

Guilt Trip
Pill Trip
Sad Trip
Bad Trip
Ego Trip
~~Ego Death~~
~~Relation~~
Ego Death
(Relation Ship)

A.T.A

26Fish

love is lonely
only
when you're in it alone

passion is love
that can't be controlled

who doesn't love Love?
who doesn't Love, love?

in its truest form
it has no form
(or formula)

it doesn't make sense

it just transmits

and that's
just it

27Fish

they came up to speak
one by one
each spoke of a love

that was matched by none

but no one could claim her
or call her their own
just spoke of the luck
to ever have known

not a tear would be shown
cuz she was finally home

Miss in love with the world
never became Mrs.

but the smile she would end with

proved nothing was missing

she died alone

but she was contented

28Fish

* a short story inspired by the Langston Hughes poem "Life is Fine"

It was very cold that day, even though the sun was shining.

Sarah woke up sooner than she had planned. The empty bottles of opioids and Tequila stared her in the face as she opened her eyes. She tried to force herself back to sleep, but the vomit rising in her throat wouldn't allow it. With all the blinds drawn in her tiny apartment it was impossible to tell what time of day it was. Sarah could care less. "I wonder if I just lay here on my back and choke on my own vomit like Jimi Hendrix... maybe that'll work," Sarah thought to herself. She chuckled at how morbid she could be and the vomit succeeded. The phone rang and she stumbled towards the bathroom. It had probably been ringing all morning. More than likely her mother calling to say, "Happy Birthday."

March 13th, Sarah's 27th birthday and the day she would have liked to be her last day on earth. "I've still got time," she figured. Sarah looked at the hair dryer and then the tub thinking how poetic it would be to be found that way; lifeless in a warm bubble bath. But it wasn't bad ass enough for her. She always considered herself to be a real rebel without a cause. "Why would you give me such a boring name like, Sarah?" she once asked her mother when she was 16. She never thought Sarah was an edgy enough name for her. "Roxanne," she said out loud as she stood and looked in the mirror, "I'm more of a Roxanne."

The phone rang again and this time she had a feeling it was him.

The same "him" who the night before she caught having sex with her best friend. She couldn't allow herself to answer the phone. She swore she would never be like her mother and let a man like her father run over her and ultimately ruin her entire existence.

"They all leave eventually," Sarah thought to herself the night before as she swallowed the poisons that were to end her so-called misery. He had been the father she never wanted, but always needed. She had given in to love, in which she always believed to be a lie.

The little piece of paper that would have been her last testimony to family and friends was neatly folded at the edge of her bed. Sarah couldn't understand why her attempt had failed, "A fucking waste of paper," she said to herself. She opened up the note which read:

"To whom it may concern,
This will be the last time I cry; the last time I put my all into a lie. I can't take the pain of a love lost...a love never had...the story of my life. Goodbye."

She chuckled a bit and said to herself, "Sarah, you're a fucking nut job." As she looked down at her ring finger where the engagement ring had been, she wondered what she had done with it in her drunken state the night before. Her eyes began to tear. In her little apartment with vomit all over her bed spread, on her 27th birthday, she was alone. She walked to the kitchen to grab a knife. "I've seen this in a movie once...it's a sure thing," she thought. Upon opening up the knife drawer she saw that there were no clean knives. "FUCK!" she screamed. A germaphobe like her mother, a dirty utensil was not an option. It wasn't suppose to be this hard to kill yourself. If only she had gotten her firearm license like she had planned, she could have shot herself and went out in true "bad ass" fashion. She had planned on buying a gun. She had planned on getting a skull tattoo on her breast. She had planned on skydiving one day, but never got around to it. Instead she lead a very safe life. Sarah was just a "Sarah." Not quite the rebel she thought she was. The reason she was still alive today.

As she fell to the kitchen floor, the cold tiles made her shiver. A jolt that reminded her she was alive. And with it, an awareness that maybe she should stay that way. Her doorbell rang. "Great" she thought as she scooped herself up.

"Happy Birthday my love!" her mother sang, bursting through the door. "Well! It looks like you celebrated early huh?!" Sarah ran to the toilet to dispose of what would be the last of her vomit from the night before. "My dear! Its 3pm! Open these blinds and let's get the day started!" Sarah wiped the throw up from her mouth and sat on the note, on the edge of her bed. "Looks like you've had a rough night," her mother laughed. Annoyed but relieved, she looked at her mother and couldn't help but smile. She paused for a moment to decide whether or not she'd tell her about all that had happened. Perhaps she'd show her the note. But instead, she just smiled and didn't say a word.

As she stood up to open the blinds like her mother had ordered, she was instantly hit by the rays of the sun. And though it was very cold that day, in that moment she was gratefully warm.

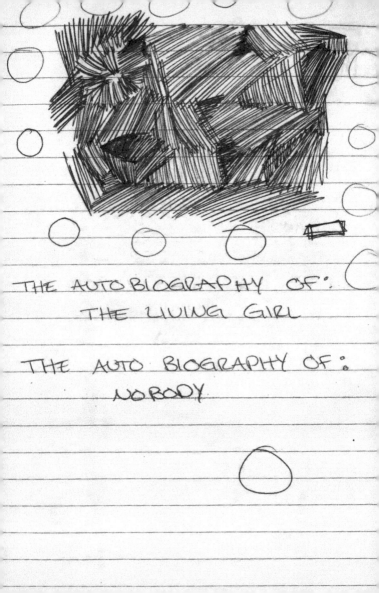

THE AUTOBIOGRAPHY OF:
THE LIVING GIRL

THE AUTO BIOGRAPHY OF:
NOBODY

29Fish

how to kill a crush:
crush him

30Fish

i have recently noticed
that when she's alone it's
more likely that she's at her best

she shines in the darkness
(a reclusive artist)

but
she is a star none the less

she is sensitive to spotlights
and sensitive to judgments

sensitive to opinions
of what she does
or doesn't

she can not dance or sing like no one is watching

when she knows in fact
that they are

they would never see
her potential to be

none the less
she was
still a star

shining brightest on the night shift
no one there to compare

praise nor blame can affect her
when no one else is there

she is scared

in a room full of people
who don't treat her like an equal
she can hear their thoughts
she is caught
they are see-through
(and evil)

so she waits
to be great

when she gets off the stage
and the night turns to day
and brings solitude

no one in the way
no one there to say
what she did that was right
or didn't do

THERE IS NOTHING HERE
CAN YOU HEAR IT?
IT IS DANGEROUS
DON'T GET NEAR IT
THE CALM MEANS
THE STORM IS SOON TO COM

31Fish

your worst (you are here) your best

32Fish

sometimes i forget to breathe
what exactly does that mean?

(don't forget to breathe, please)

33Fish

yes
even her
a life that is envied
wishes she were
just
a bit more pretty
maybe even taller
and a lot less skinny
and at least two shades
lighter
or darker
or any...
anything more relatable
for
belonging
or fitting
into a world
with a
long history of
division

(i was never good at math...especially long division)

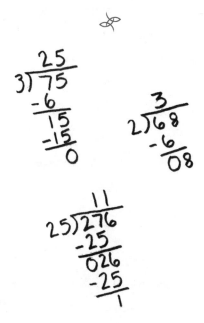

maybe something is wrong
with me
I think I am RIGHT
Don't know what to write
my LETTERS are WEIRD.
I have no aim
no focus
goal less
go less. stop more
I'm in it for the long
RUN.

The wrong one.
Melody RUNS DEEP
I FEEL it in the ~~my~~ beat
of the heart, that WEAPS
And the EYES that CRY
are not always to be BELIEVE

THE HEART THAT WEEPS

34Fish

i am so sorry

i am so strange

it's how i was made
i can't change

this is my way

(to follow my way)

go crazy

'til you get to sane

35Fish

we're not in love
we are on drugs

we are not happy
we're high

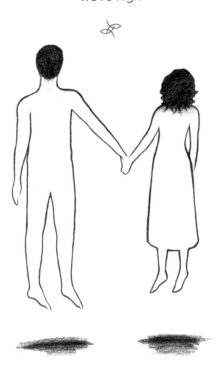

YOU'RE in YOUR OWN WAY
again

GET OUT of YOUR OWN WAY

a WAY
AWAY
a WAY

WHERE THERE'S a WHEEL
THERE'S a WAY
AND I must say
This is turning into
something good.
LiKE I KNOW it would
AND I think ~~ass~~ I should
FucK it up
Just ~~because~~
I KNOW all things
~~Eventually~~, do ~~and~~
~~BETTER~~ me than you
~~Rather~~ me than you

36Fish

have fun without me
don't miss me when i'm gone
rejoice in my absence
and sing happy songs

please burn my body
and take it to sea
then have a boat party
and have fun without me

don't hold on to memories
do not reminisce
don't regret what u didn't say
do not hope
do not wish

spread my ashes near South Point
on the green sand beach

celebrate my freedom

and have fun without me

The world's a fuckin mess
it's gone to shit
and i am every bit apart of
i may have started it

i try to find the brighter side
tan elevated
higher side
~~idea~~ is out of sight

OBLIVION
WISH I WOULD GO BACK
I COULD GO BACK to NO ONE
OBLIVION
WISH I WOULD GO BACK
I COULD GO BACK to Nothing

37Fish

i've been going through withdrawals

making more withdrawals

than deposits

buying winter coats

for the skeletons in my closet

38Fish

in the middle of somewhere
on the edge of rejection
i took my self back
and i started accepting
that life is just moment
to moment
to moment
there's no use in dwelling
you can not control it
or hold it
or pause it
or call it
your own
there's no destination
you're already home

The girl with
The heart that weeps
and the eyes that bleed

Completely incomplete....
Hearts on sleeves
are pet peeves.....,
Counting sheeps to sleep.

Retreat!
Retreat!
Back inside the tiny bubble.
No one knows you, ~~please stay~~ PLEASE STAY
~~No one knows you~~ . HUMBLE

~~(that loves chasing?)~~

THE BELL THAT DOESN'T RING

THE BELL that doesn't ring

THE BELL that DOES NOT
RING

39Fish

please come take me away from me

4OFish

he was all of the good things
i thought i deserved

(some type of test from the Gods)

he wasn't willing
and i wasn't ready

(but we were in love with the odds)

~~GOTTA GET A GRIP~~

GOTTA GET A GRIP

~~GOTTA~~

GOTTA GET A GRIP

TRIPPIN

BRAIN SAILS :)

Brain cells!

Brains SELL

BLAME SELF :)

PAW HELPS!

CRASH AND BURN

B's & H's

FOCUS!

NOPE :-

GOOD BYE

FOR NOW

FOR EVER

NEVER.

41Fish

not just L.A.
not just Black
and Japanese
or 30 percent that
or anything in between

i am not just
a product of things

but a product of all
the kings and the queens

i am the collective

of divinity

the earth,
the sky,
the stars,
and the seas.

42Fish

the curator killed the creator :-(

43Fish

July 19, 2012
3:16 pm

writing has always been my therapy
i never really talked about things
when I was younger i'd write in my diary and leave it around so that someone would read it
so that they'd know what I was going through
without me having to talk about it out loud

i'm on the way to San Francisco
for a turn around trip
to say good bye to my uncle
my father's brother who is on his death bed
dying from cancer

there is absolutely no love like the love between siblings
i grew up in a house hold where I was the youngest of five
same mom and dad
we grew up sharing everything
doing everything together
i couldn't wait for the day I could get away and have my own space

often times it was just me and Miyagi and Jahi
and then just me and Miyagi downstairs at my grandmother's house
chillin
watching Disney movies on VHS
arguing
staying out of each others business
big brother/little sister stuff

Dear #4,
When I had Nami and no place of my own to stay
all 3 of us would sleep on ur futon
I always ended up on the floor
when we first found out u had a brain tumor
you were so strong
you made it ok
you were still you
joking and smiling
it was easy to forget
it was easy to stay away and do my own thing
easy to assume we'd grow old together

and that all the ideas we shared would come to fruition
and that you'd be here for Nami's prom and graduation

but
just yesterday
heard the nurses say
you only have
5 to 7 days
if that's the case
It may be the same for me

i'm debating

i can not make a distinction between the two of us

see,
i'm 24 and you're 26
and all throughout school kids assumed we were twins
truth is,
we are best friends
Bart and Lisa Simpson

Miyagi, you taught me
how to fight
both physically and mentally
taught me to laugh from my gut
and how to tell the best jokes

i prepared my whole life to lose a father or mother
but never a brother.
and everyone says,
"you aren't alone"
but the truth is,
i am
because they haven't had you as a brother
like I have

we called you baby Jesus
because as a baby
in a school play at Miyoko and Jamila's school
you played the role of baby Jesus
and you grew up to be a Saint in your own way
i can't think of one person who you haven't made laugh uncontrollably
or one baby or animal that wasn't naturally drawn to you
i wrote and recorded a song for you
that i've been too nervous to play for you

asking you to not give up ur fight
and to stay with us longer
but i realize I am being selfish
i am everything I am because of you

you deserve the very best
that maybe this world can't offer you
so I won't complain and say that life isn't fair
i know that your best friend Brian is there waiting for you
and I know you'll be waiting for me too

ages, phases and stages
no ends
everything is always changing
i'm finally doing the things i've always dreamed
i can feel you giving me that extra push

Miyagi,
there is no such thing as losing you
you will always be with me
we don't die, we multiply
to infinity and beyond ∞

Love, #5

New Balance

ost of us are angry
ost of us are STRANGELY
ore ALIKE THAN WE'D LIKE
O BELIEVE

Most of us are EMPTY
Most of us are SIMPLY
~~Irorprooofeeond~~
ore ALIVE ~~coroo~~ IN THE SCENES
of OUR DREAMS

Then THERE'S YOU
YOU ~~got~~ somethin
I ~~been~~ wantin, ohh
Life's a challenge,
with no balance, ohh

salvage   new
                you

I always wanted to star
in the play ALWAYS But
I ~~always~~ was the
narrattor.

I DON'T ~~FEEL~~ PRETTY
I Don't ~~feel~~ Any!
thing

"The couple that comes
~~together~~
stays together."

:)

44Fish

i want to smile at strangers
and laugh w/ danger
befriend and put an end to anger

break the chains
and chase away doubt
run nude around the city and shout
"FREE LOVE! FREE LOVE!"

it's being held captive by the thieves of
compassion
and they want a ransom
but I'm not understanding
cuz all love is free love
in it's truest fashion

and if you're gonna love
i mean really, truly love
then you gotta be love
be free, love!
FREE LOVE!

45Fish

to the man i never met
i'm gonna try to keep this short and simple
i will never forget you
and there are millions just like me
that feel the same
the brain you spoke of sparking
you did just that
to a generation
your image
your sound
your words
your message
your energy
unafraid to be yourself and make mistakes
too many of us are scared to look crazy and contradict ourselves
but we all are walking, breathing contradictions
only some of us are brave enough to contradict ourselves out loud
and be the real
multidimensional creatures that we were born to be
"ever changing
never twice the same"
you are proof that one ordinary individual
no super power
just words
can change the world
and for that
i thank you
i've never met you
nor am I old enough to have enjoyed you in your prime
all i have are pictures
interviews
poems
all clues to who you were
help me understand who I am

light worker
i am your child
i am like you
i am proud
when you say thug life
i know what you mean
i feel like my family has been thuggin our whole lives
i feel like no one understands what it feels like to have a gun in their face
at 5
to have their house burn down
or to wait hours in county lines
or to watch my closest brother die
to be hopeless
but still find reasons to smile
but everyone does understand
because we all go through shit
and we're all suffering
because we're all in the gutter
and we're still here
so when you say "Keep Your Head Up"
i know what you mean
and though i've never met you
i will never forget you
so fuck what everyone else says or thinks
i am thankful for what you've
inspired me to be

- sincerely, Jhené Chilombo

I took a trip
aboard a ship
~~with~~ no captain
But
~~And~~ you were my anchor

There ~~were~~ ~~poison~~ poison
And ~~poison~~ ~~strangers~~ /Deme
AND Rhyms with no rea~~
AND STRANGERS

But there was no Danger

WAS   BRIGHTER
FIGHTER

46Fish

soil slathered with concrete
trees systematically placed
competing for a useless prize
in a completely made up race

the root of the problem is
our roots were cut
before we learned to live
and now we're disconnected from
the essence of
what is

47Fish

i asked him "why?"
and he replied,
"cuz you're so pretty when you cry."

NEAT NEAT NEAT

WHAT WOULD YOU LIKE ME TO SAY?
FOR SAFE TRAVELS ON LIFE'S
MANY TRIPS
    I think I'm forgetting
    how to do this
WHERE am I now?
    I forgot everything

Just let it flow, I suppose
time ~~TRAVEL~~

I want to learn more.
I want to see more?
I'm not sure.
I can never make up my mind.
    That's my problem
    and my way

Find a better way

48Fish

the end was coming
the people were running
heard sirens
i turned on the news

evacuation required
there was lightning and fires
but I sat there
waiting for you

the windows were breaking
the Earth began shaking
as i sat there making your bed
i smiled as i did it
and laughed reminiscing
memories with you filled my head

the house started flooding
the water was rushing
to my feet
then my waist
then my neck

i said a small prayer
thanked the Woman upstairs
and took my last
final breath

got up to the gates
got into the line
heard them call my name
time after time

they came out to get me
(which the angels seldom do)
and welcomed me home

but to tell the truth

i turned them down
i had to refuse

i'll keep heaven waiting

for you

sweet oblivion
sweet oblivious

sweet oblivion
I remember when
I was in your warm embrace
without a trace
without a name
or face

Sweet oblivion
you are the star I wish upon
to be reborn as your unborn
as your sweet pile of nothing

how sweet it is
oblivious
admist a world
where everyone is
somebody

sweet oblivion
I remember when, I miss it when
I was nobody

49Fish

you ever wonder
how wonderful it would be
to be as
content
and free
as a tree?

i think
animals were impatient plants

bad seeds

who couldn't keep still
and just had to leave

disconnected from the Earth's soil
evolved into humans
and in return
ruined

their capability of truly growing
incapable of truly knowing

chasing the wind
rather than being still in it
racing w/the Sun
rather than feeling it

consider the things
the plants have seen
and been through
and gained
by staying the same

yet accepting the change

one day
i hope to be
as grounded
as stable
as patient
and keen

as the free flowing
ever growing
all knowing
tree

Paia   Jan. 2, 2014
                        occur

passed Paia Brilliant
Half way to Hana
Half Baked to Hana

        Seven Sacred Pools
                (Polls)
                    of weed :)

in the PRAM
& LIVING WILD   on the RIGHT
WE ARE THE   BAND

DREAMERS OF   TO THE WRONG
    THE NIGHTMARE   PLACE

I AM THE
        CHILD   Rulers of OUR own
BURY ME BY   Land
    the Black Sand
        Beach

5OFish

a short ode to blue

blue is my favorite color
if i'm feeling blue
then I'm feeling wonder
full of life like the sky and the ocean

blue is my favorite emotion

full of life
like the test with the lines

there were two

they were blue

they were you

and you gave my life some direction

blue is my favorite conception

51Fish

two fish
different directions
one is accepting
one is rejecting
one is a curse
the other's a blessing
while one is the worst
the other's the best thing
and there is no resting
between the two
it's either
it's or

but she'll never choose
hopeful and bruised
sure, but confused
one fish
with a wish
split into two

52Fish

(a haiku for Nami)

daughter of the wave
crashes against the shore and
carries me away

RANDOM NOTES

KEEP ~~it~~ FOR YOURSELF.

~~THE~~ BEGINNING ~~of~~ pain.

When one thought LEADS
to another

~~WHERE~~ DO I END UP?

~~REDRUM?~~

IN SANE?

PLAIN. No such thing as pla
AND SIMPLE IS REALLY
EVERTHING
AT IT'S BASIS
IT'S BASIC

~~TRANSLATION:~~ ~~xxxxxxxxxxxxx~~

~~xxxxxxxxxxxxx~~

~~xxxxxxxxxxx~~

Do you know what I'm sayin?

LIFE IS JUST A SONG
LEARN THE WORDS
AND SING ALONG
        GIVE UNTIL
        YOU GET ALONG
    RIGHT THE WRONGS

            WRITE
WHERE YOU ARE.

            RIGHT
WHERE YOU ARE.

    BEAUTY. TIME. LIFE.
HADOWS. BLURRY. MOVEMENT. CIRCLES
INGING. PRETTY. LEMONS.
    CRAZY. SAYING. STOP.

53Fish

i'm trying
i'm trying
i'm trying

i'm tired

54Fish

for a limited time only, always

PLEASE STOP SKIPPING PAGES
what if I only told you
everything I've ever wanted to
no one else
Only you?

what if I only told you
All the things
I wanted to say?

Stop thinking about it
WRITE WITHOUT direction
without a destination

CREATIVE CREATED EMPTY MIND

CREATE A CREATIVE EMPTY MIND
Empty mine
no GOLD
WHO TOLD YOU?

55Fish

i need more responsibilities

to be more responsible

is that how it works?
is that possible?

well it's probably

just me being me

i'm always in need
i'm impossible

56Fish

maybe you're right
i'm exactly what you think of me

maybe you're wrong
who knows

but for a fact

i'm more than what you know of me

and less than what you would suppose

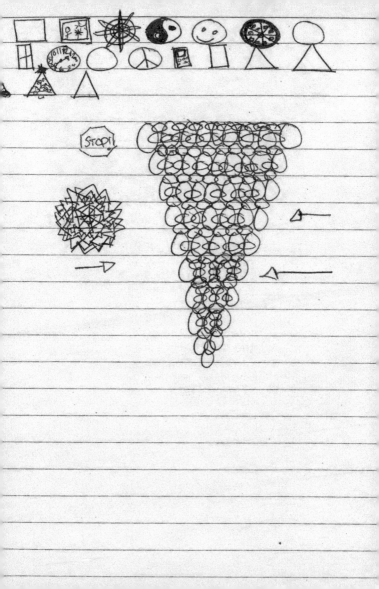

STOP!

57Fish

nights are colder
days seem longer
pray it only makes me stronger
stopping at green lights
running the red
mourning the living
and envy the dead
crying in silence
thinking out loud
i'm growing older
and into a child
more suffering and pain
the greater i became
discovering me
for the first time
again

58Fish

up late
need space

i'm not sure how i should ask for it

nights off
lights off

how did i end up alone?

more time
more faith

i can't seem to get a hold of it

test fate
best case

i'll find a way on my own

Nothing to say
Everything to do

Lightining in a Bottle

~~I~~ pissed my pants
~~Thanks.~~
~~Tired.~~
Trippin
Trip is over

~~Sober~~

Roller coaster
~~thank you for the ligh~~

In sight. ~~////~~

WHAT'S ALL THIS FOR

tate will eat you up inside.

SELF-inflicted sickness

I'm trippin.

When did I become this old
(inflicted)

over crowded with uncert~

every thing I SEE , it

WORRIES ME.

I keep thinking my dreams

are ~~REAL~~ memories

I can't get my self

out of my misery.

no tellin will no L
How long will it last? tell
will you catch me
when I crash?

"SOMEWHERE BETWEEN"
FACT & FANTASY

TIME TO TRIP

TRIP TIME

Time to TRip

59Fish

we need each other.

60Fish

my grandpa teddy's mom
was the first person i knew i loved for sure
when i was 4 or 5 years old
it was love at first sight really
with her fluffy white hair and soft wrinkly skin
her smile wasn't forced
and never seemed to fade

peaceful
petite
like the doll of my dreams
i never cared too much for barbies

she was different
and better
than any person i had ever seen
a delicate wisdom
so serene

i knew her as soon as i met her

i lost her as soon as i met her

i was told
because she was old
she may not wake up
the next day

so i stayed awake
hoping that if i didn't sleep
that i could keep her up
w/ me

the morning came
the adults explained
she would stay asleep forever

but i had an idea

i had learned about prayer
in church with Grandma Essie
so i thought
that i would start there

so i ran to the backyard and
shouted out loud
"God! You can bring her back through the clouds!

If she drops from the sky...
i won't be frightened or cry
i just want her back right now.

Amen"

i waited
with patience
i stared at the Sun

i sat with the Sun
til my skin changed tones

there was no reply
but it was such a pretty day still

i learned how to lose that day

i asked my father where her body went
as a doctor he explained
as a Buddhist her body was burned

i stared at the fire
where the fireplace was
completely in awe
and concerned

we practiced Buddhist ceremony
everyday before her service
i learned about incense and bowing

i met Japanese family
who sat with my family
in awe that
this spectrum of people
were family

i learned about family that day

i don't remember crying

but i do remember thinking
(and i haven't stopped thinking since)

about love
about loss
about life
and it's purpose

its perfect
but doesn't make sense

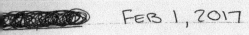 FEB 1, 2017

I am afraid
I am not good enough
I deserve anything great
I can not stop comparing

I afraid I will never get it
right. Im afraid I will give up
before my time.

I am afraid I am losing my se
to my addictions
I am afraid I am addicted
to everything.

I need so much attention
but also, so much space

I am afraid that I will
push everyone away

I am envious
I am selfish
I am lazy
I can't focus
I am inconsistent
I am confused
I am too skinny
I am too concerned with what others think
I am over stimulated
I am too needy
I am consumed with thous of not being able to compar or compete
I am lost
I am uninspired
I am tired
I can't sleep
I am disconnected

61Fish

an ode to opioids!

only optimistic
when the opioid kicks in

to avoid
consequences
of selfish decisions

opioids
to destroy
my vision

opioids
to kill the noise
and fill the voids
to feel the joy
to
drown out the voices
that make better choices
i down them with poisons

its torture

an ode to opioids!

62Fish

smiling at strangers
and
flirting w/ danger
for the remainder of

this life

and never ever

ever ever

EVER

thinking twice

63Fish

for inspirational purposes only

64Fish

i once told a stranger i met

"the more that you know me,
the more you'll forget.
the closer we grow,
the stranger i get"

he doesn't get it quite yet

65Fish

a fish out of water
when she's not in love

so she falls in order
and just
because

she wants to live longer
and get what she gives

a love everlasting

an outlandish
myth

66Fish

please
do not stray from the path
it's been written in pen
on the grid
do the math
every bend is in
the decisions you make
so follow the flow
for goodness sake

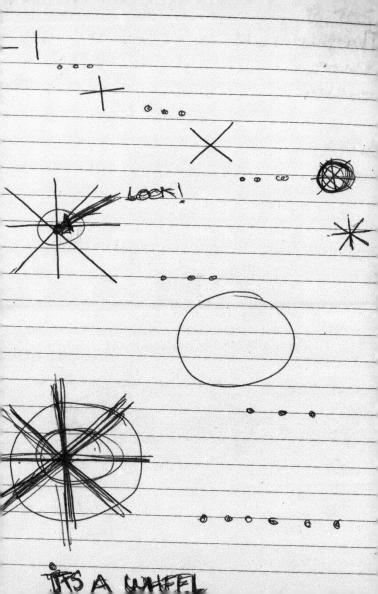

Look!

IT'S A WHEEL

67Fish

there is beauty in balance
the triumphs
and
struggles

this is like this

because that's like
the other

68Fish

Can't Really Understand the Situation, Honestly

the rush of the CRUSH
really bothers me

MOST OF US ARE HURTING
MOST OF US ARE SEARCHING
FOR SOME ONE TO LOVE US
SOME ONE WHO UNDER

MOST THE THE time I'm
Fighting
Multiple voices in side me
THEY ALL RESIDE IN THE
my head IN THE

Most of us cant take i
Most the time we're
faking

Most of us are
fabricated
Most the time I smile
I'm fakin
MOST OF US THAT REAL
UNTIL WE'RE DEAD

Most of us

MOST OF ALL

MOST THE TIME

SO MOST OF US

THEN THERE'S YOU,
YOU BRING SILENCE
TO MY VIOLENT
TRUTH

69Fish

i found another grey hair today
but i was not bothered at all
i feel like i earned it
i'm better
i'm wiser

i'm leveling up
over all

i'm becoming my mother
my beautiful mother
who taught me
with age
comes might!

i'm becoming my mother
my beautiful mother
i am LOVE
in the flesh

what a sight!

70Fish

i still have so much more to say...

(a page to fill in the blanks)

About the Author

Jhené Aiko Efuru Chilombo was born on March 16, 1988, in Los Angeles, California. Jhené began writing poetry at 6 years old. At 13, she signed to a major record label and began her career as a recording artist. Today, she is a mother of one, a three-time Grammy-nominated singer/songwriter, and a poet. *2Fish* is Jhené's first published book.